Abstract

This book looks at Augusto Boal's Theatre of the Oppressed and the wider framework in which it operates. The focus is on the semiotic aspect of theatre. There are a number of elements in the theatre that follow codes and conventions. When conceiving theatre as a language these can be subverted in order to make particular statements. Boal's work draws from Brecht's Marxist drama and Paulo Freire's 'Pedagogy of the Oppressed'. The concept of 'Dialectics' is a key term in Brecht's work. Indeed, Boal conceives oppression as the absence of dialogue. Boal's aesthetic language developed in Brazil's military coup environment. At the time the challenge was to provide people with a system of symbols that could pair the written and spoken language. Then, Boal formulated the concept of 'spect-actor'. Some voices claim that the method has become dogmatic. At the present, Boal is no icon of oppression.

A number of theatre companies specialise in tackling specific social issues that lead to isolation and social apartheid. This is supported by a social policy and funding bodies that seek social cohesion through these kind of schemes.

Contents

Introduction

This book looks at the Theatre of the Oppressed and explores the possibilities of drama as an agent of social change. The critical analysis of the theory and practice of Augusto Boal's theatre demonstrates the suitability of the method to deal with social issues.

Indeed there is a significant number of organisations using innovative drama techniques for social purposes. However, it is essential to interrogate the sudden increase in number of this type of company and assess their achievements as well as their failings. The social inclusion agenda is one of the components that has triggered the spread of Boal's discourse.

Augusto Boal's theatre is a universal language that contests discourses of domination and offers a democratic arena to question and transform the *status quo*. This is the essence of the Theatre of the Oppressed (TO). Rehearse it. Play it. See it. Change it. Augusto Boal's TO encourages a social revolution that starts on stage. This approach focuses on the sociological aspects of theatre rather than on its aesthetic or artistic aspirations. A pragmatics of theatre that makes a move towards 'the people' and has a number of implications regarding issues of resistance to power amongst others.

Certainly, the Theatre of the Oppressed, as any form of community theatre, claims to give a voice to the voiceless. By doing so, it transforms the nature of the dramatic discourse. Audience and actors. Plot and story. 'I' and 'you', the classic *deixis*, that establishes space and characters. As a language, theatre displays a collection of rules and conventions. These are the result of cultural formation and therefore, text and context become equally relevant.

4

Encoding and decoding a text varies from one community to another since cultural values and perceptions also vary. Subversion does not always show the same expression. Raymond William's 'oppositional performance'[1] is one notion disclosing unlimited appearances. To identify a community's references assists in understanding their struggle. Thus, theatre calls for semiotic analysis. Here structuralist and formalist study come into play. Theatre is a two-way communication that reveals the wide range of binary oppositions entrenched within the dialectic of power relations Oppressed and oppressors. A straightforward coercion that exhibits multiple dimensions. Indeed, it is important to question the suitability of this expression for other revolutions. That is to say, whether this expression suits different contexts or rather calls for alterations of the original model. Indeed, the circumstances of oppression may vary and so the TO or other similar types of performance can be adapted to the situation.

Boal's theatre started in Brazil's early 1970s where coercion was not a subtle one. at the time Latin American dictatorships transformed the violation of human rights into a daily practice. The need for finding a suitable expression was a matter of acknowledging one's existence. Theatre as a sign-system is a vehicle for communication for people lacking one. This is a significant change since in a way, theatre serves as a medium to bring particular ideas into life, to awake consciousness and to produce change off stage. Beyond the dividing lines present in classic theatre, Boal seeks to fully explore the possibilities that theatre offers, and among others formulates 'legislative theatre' in which theatre attempts to make a fundamental change in the legal system. Indeed, Boal's rhetoric is loaded with resistance warnings since:[2]

---

[1] Raymond Williams *Culture* (London:Fontana, 1981), 85 quoted in Baz Kershaw *The Politics of Performance* (London:Routledge, 1992), 6
[2] Augusto Boal *Legislative Theatre* (Oxon: Routledge, 1998), cover

'(…) to transgress, to break the conventions, to enter the mirror of a theatrical fiction, rehearse forms of struggle and then return to reality with the images of their desires. This discontent was the genesis of legislative theatre in which the citizen makes the law through the legislator'.

Chapter 1 looks at 'theatre' as a text and provides an insight to its main elements. Thus, it is argued that in an ideologically loaded context in theatrical deixis 'I'- 'You', that traditionally determines spaces and speakers, becomes a platform in which to identify power relations and other binary oppositions that imply the us/them relationship. Boal deals with macro social aspect. Following the *Brechtian* tradition he dismisses Aristotle's catharsis and instead gives the spectator a big part to play in meaning making, he is both the encoder and decoder of the text.

Chapter 2 focuses on Boal's theories and practice evaluating the influences of Paulo Freire and Bertolt Brecht in his work. Likewise, this chapter raises the idea of Boal as an institution and examines the backlash of his status as a "celebrity".

Chapter 3 contextualises the TO in the UK, provides an over view of the history of alternative theatre and gives an account of some of the organisations implementing the method.

Chapter 4 includes an account of the methodology

Lastly, Chapter 5 looks at the actual praxis of the TO and presents comments and opinions of professional theatre practitioners in the UK and the world.

Chapter 1   Theatre as a language

This chapter will introduce some of the basic theatrical elements that are later revisited by the Theatre of the Oppressed. The focus is on the semiotic aspect of theatre as well as the interaction between audience and actors. There are a number of elements in theatre such as plot, actors, stage directions and so on that follow rules and conventions. When approaching theatre as a language these can be subverted in order to make particular statements. Indeed, as Aston and Savona (1991)[3] state: (…) a text which subverts expectations may usefully serve to reawaken our perceptions of literary construction and the devices which underpin it…a 'deviant' text, through its abuse of dramatic conventions, draws our attention to sign-systems of structure'. As an example, to perform outside the theatre building is to break with such standards and changes alike can highlight the ideological aspect of a performance. Nevertheless, rules and conventions are not universal since they are shaped by the cultural formation of the community they belong to. Similarly, there are techniques of 'defamiliarisation' that drag the spectator to an unfamiliar space in which to question the very essence of the pre-established rules of a cultural expression like theatre. Bertolt Brecht challenges a cathartic audience and instead promoted the so-called 'political theatre'.

Semiotics. Ferdinand De Saussure

In order to understand theatre as a language it is useful to look at some basic principles of semiotics. Swiss linguist Ferdinand De Saussure described semiotics as the 'science which studies the life of signs at the heart of social life'.[4] In other words, semiology examines the way meaning is socially constructed. De Saussure states:[5]

---

[3] Elaine Aston, and George Savona *Theatre as a sign-system* (London: Routledge, 1991)
[4] Ferdinand De Saussure *Course in General Linguistics* (Paris: Editions de Payot, 1972) Available at: http://www.marxists.org/reference/subject/philosophy/works/fr/saussure.htm
[5] Ibid.

'We can say that the object to be studied is the hoard deposited in the brain of each one of us; doubtless this hoard, in any individual case, will never turn out to be absolutely complete. We can say that language always works through a language', without that, it does not exist. The language, in turn is quite independent of the individual; it cannot be a creation of the individual-, it is essentially social; it presupposes the collectivity.'

Thus, De Saussure refers to a social language that can be reflected on a book, a film, a song or a play. Semioticians refer to all those items as 'texts'. The receiver of a message or text is a reader. The reader engages in an active practice when he/she decodes a text. However, the decoding of any text is a practice socially and culturally determined.

As language is a social product so is the perception of reality that is governed by the same codes and conventions. John Fiske explains:[6]

'Reality' is always encoded, or rather the only way we can perceive and make sense of reality is by the codes of our culture. There may be an objective, empiricist reality out there, but there is no universal, objective way of perceiving and making sense of it. What passes for reality in any culture is the product of the culture's codes, so 'reality' is always already encoded, it is never 'raw'.

Under Fiske's argument it follows that a discursive practice such as theatre is conditioned by the reality it presents or questions. A play such as Coriolanus[7], a tragedy by William Shakespeare, can be interpreted as promoting or denying fascism. Attention has been drawn to the element of duality operating within theatre since according to Alter theatre makes:

[6] Jon Fiske *Understanding Popular Culture* (London: Routledge, 1987), 4, 5
[7] Augusto Boal *Theatre of the Oppressed* (London: Pluto Press, 1979), 174

reference to a story that takes place in a mental space outside the stage; display of real performances on the stage.'[8]

This statement illustrates very well the semiotic aspect of theatre in which the audience members decode signs according to their mental repertoire of references. The preferred meaning of a text is established through particular standards relying on the cultural values of a given group, community or society. As such, texts can be ideologically loaded and thus seek to promulgate, consolidate or subvert particular discourses, As Kershaw (1992) states:[9]

'(…) move beyond formalist analysis- which treats theatre as if it were independent of its social and political environment – and consider performances as a cultural construct and as a means of cultural production (…) seen in their full cultural milieu: in relation to the aesthetic movements of which they are part in relation to the institutional structures of the arts; cultural formations they inhabit. Culture is saturated with discourses of power'

and he follows:[10]

'… a show celebrating the IRA is one thing on the Falls road, quite another thing in a British army camp. (…) the context of performance directly affects its perceived meaning'. The socio-cultural complexion of the audience, its sense of community (or lack of it) is the most crucial factor in evoking the contextuality of a text'.

Indeed, when looking at theatre's discourse of power one encounters the central division between stage and audience, this dividing line derives from ancient Greek's aristocracy theatre. The social hierarchy is taken to the stage and two categories of citizens are created. Actors and passive audience. There is a subcategory of actors, the protagonists and the

---

[8] Alter, *A Sociosemiotic Theory of Theatre* (USA: University of Pennsylvania Press, 1990), 41
[9] Baz Kershaw *The Politics of Performance* (London: Routledge, 1992), 6
[10] Baz Kershaw *The Politics of Performance* (London: Routledge, 1992), 33

chorus. The audience or mass is confronted to their reality while they play role by never being able to change the action on stage. As Alter puts it: 'Under the disguises of a role, a truth is manifested; and the reality of the stage merges magically with the fiction in which it is mirrored'.[11]

Audience and Actors

The nature of the relationship between audience and actors has traditionally been a limited one. The clearly defining walls between actors and spectators allow little room for exchange. Theatre as a language allows a two-way communication, however the gaze is always placed on the actors side, where the action is located. These elements first emerged within the Greek tragedy and the classic forms of theatre. Over time they have been reformulated and addressed from different stances. Similarly, ideology does play a big part in defining performance methods. Thus, in regards to the audience there has been a conception, or perhaps a misconception, that attributes a passive function to the audience. Within conventional theatre the spectators might not be as participative as in other forms of theatre, however, the relationship between actor and audience is subtle yet present. Needless to say, this two-way communication is determined by a ritualistic inaction between senders and receivers of signs that allow limited reactions. However limited, these reactions are the feedback that actors seek during their performance. The audience display signs like:[12] 'voices, laughter, hisses, foot-stamping, applause...etc'. the underlying purpose is beyond storytelling, indeed as Alter states:[13]

> 'when they display referential signs, they certainly aim at telling a story; but also want to elicit a response from the audience: an emotional reaction, an expansion or change of ideas, a determination to improve the world.'

[11] Alter, *A Sociosemiotic Theory of Theatre* (USA: University of Pennsylvania Press, 1990), 41
[12] Alter, A Sociosemiotic theory of Theatre (USA: University of Pennsylvania Press, 1990), 265
[13] Ibid.

It is interesting to note that the 'emotional reaction' is more on the catharsis principle seeking to arouse feelings. Nevertheless 'change of ideas' and 'determination to improve the world' is close to forms of theatre that encourage more than the audience's sounded signs and their full involvement with the performance.

The complicity of the audience is achieved through mechanisms of Empathia and Catharsis. Through Empathia the spectator feels and thinks like the character he/she is watching. There is no emotional detachment and as a result the spectator has no ability to ask a critical stand point nor to question any of the ideological points raised during the performance. Boal mentions Brecht's comment on the hypnotic power of Empathia and its assistance preserving control on the people. Boal comments:[14]

'Brecht writing about Aristotle, made a suggestion. He began by saying that this empathia thing was all right for the ruling classes, who even ruled their characters' ideology; but it wouldn't suit the workers, for it helped them perpetuate exploitation.'

Bertolt Brecht and the Marxist Drama

Bertolt Brecht was the pioneer of the so-called 'Epic theatre', which challenged the traditional concept of Empathia and its cathartic effect.[15] Instead, he encouraged the spectator to take a critical perspective of the actions performed on stage. Subsequently, the audiences would use this ability to identify social problems and to make real changes. Brecht's revolutionary ideas contest contemporary theatre practices and inaugurate a distinctive political theatre. For the first time the spectator contributes to meaning making of the text.

Brecht suggests that the essence of Marxist drama reviews questions of time and space. In this context a Marxist drama is a drama where dialectical materialism is performed. Unlike,

---

[14] Augusto Boal Theatre of the Oppressed (London: Pluto Press, 1979), 84
[15] Epic is the term most applied to Brecht's dramatic work

naturalistic theatre the audience does not disappear along with the 'fourth wall'. Brecht's actors address directly their audience. Nevertheless, this audience is not an indiscriminate mass of people, it is a group of distinct individuals. Brecht encourages his actors:[16]

'To think of their audience as a divided group of friends and enemies, rich and poor, and to divide their audience accordingly by addressing themselves to one part of the audience now, to another part the next moment'

The concept of 'Dialectics' is a key term in Brecht's work and it is informed by the texts of Marx, Lenin and Mao Tse-tung.[17] Brecht often cites: 'the philosophers have only interpreted the world, the point is to change it'.[18]

His dramatic theory is within the line of thought of social transformation. Brecht's theatre has a number of alienation strategies that do not allow the audience to be fully absorbed by the story presented to them. Brecht's audience is able to critically analyse the text they are watching and realise the fictional quality to it. Brecht's alienation effects seek to make events strange so that the audience can question their rationale. The individual is conceived in relation to his/her inclusion in the collective narrative. In the following quote Brecht explains how to stimulate the audience's awareness:[19]

'to historicise and negate the common place and taken-for-granted, to prise open social and ideological contradictions, and so both demonstrate and provoke an awareness of the individual's place in a concrete social narrative'.

---

[16] Marowitz et al. (eds.) *The Encore Reader* (London: Methuen, 1965): 148 quoted in Margaret Eddershaw *Performing Brecht* (London: Routledge 1996), 22
[17] 'The dialectical drama' (1931), 'Dialectics in the theatre' (1948-55)
[18] Marx quoted in Peter Thompson & Glendyr Sacks (eds.) *The Cambridge companion to Brecht* (Cambridge: Cambridge University Press 1994), 186
[19] Peter Thompson & Glendyr Sacks (eds.) The Cambridge companion to Brecht (Cambridge: Cambridge University Press 1994), 186

The aim of 'historicization' is to demonstrate the Marxist idea that the individual is determined by the conditions that surround him/her:[20]

> 'Brecht called this practice 'historicization' and believed one could best adopt a critical attitude toward one's society if the present social arrangements and institutions were viewed as historical, transitory, and subject to change'

The techniques of 'making strange' are the first step to 'negate the common place and taken-for-granted', Aston looks at Brecht's 'The mother' and his techniques of 'making strange' the audience's expectations. The text introduces the character as a 'worker's mother' and a 'worker's wife'. The character's identity is defined by her association with male figures. This fact highlights the submissive feature of the character and raises controversial issues such as the inflexibility of the social class system. From a particular example Brecht reaches universal conflicts. As Aston (1991) states:[21]

> 'this violates the convention of a major, named characters as a focus of interest in themselves. In this way, Brecht opens in with an analysis of oppression in terms of class and gender, rather than in terms of the struggles of an individual.'

There are techniques of defamiliarisation that assist in turning away from Empathia and encourage a more participative and critical view of the performance, these techniques work by breaking conventions or standardised rules related to plot, characters or any theatrical element. In a way, the techniques of alienation violate traditional devices and might for example display a no-ending of a play. They work by violating the routine of a given community. Aston explains:[22]

---

[20] Betty Nance Weber and Hubert Heinen (eds.) *Bertolt Brecht Political theory and literary practice* (Manchester: Manchester University Press, 1980), 31
[21] Elaine Aston and George Sovana, *Theatre as sign-system* (London: Routledge, 1991), 32
[22] Elaine Aston and George Sovana, Theatre as sign-system (London: Routledge, 1991), 31

(…the combination and transposition of formal properties were essential to the purpose of art: to defamiliarise and de-automatise our perceptions of the world, jaded through habitualisation'

A clear example of how these techniques work are found in Eugene Ionesco's (1958) 'The bald soprano'.[23] Ionescos' work belongs to the Theatre of the Absurd, a category that is not discussed on this occasion, however, it is a good example to illustrate ways of disrupting expected conventions. The following section draws attention to an apparent incongruous dialogue that reflect on the pointlessness communication of modern societies:[24]

MRS. SMITH: Mrs. Parker knows a Rumanian grocer by the name of Popesco Rosenfeld, who has just come from Constantinople. He is a great specialist in yoghurt. He has a diploma from the school of yoghurt-making in Adrianople. Tomorrow I shall buy a large pot of native Rumanian yoghurt from him. One doesn't often find such things here in the suburbs of London.

MR. SMITH: *[continues to read, clicks his tongue.]*

MRS. SMITH: Yoghurt is excellent for the stomach, the kidneys the appendicitis, and apotheosis. It was Doctor Mackenzie-King who told me that, he's the one who takes care of the children of our neighbours, the Johns. He's a good doctor. One can trust him. He never prescribes any medicine that he's not tried out on himself first. Before operating on Parker, he had his own liver operated on first, although he was not the least bit ill.

MR. SMITH: But how does it happen that the doctor pulled through while Parker died?

[23] http://vtheatre.net/biomechanics/scenes.html
[24] Ibid.

MRS. SMITH: Because the operation was successful in the doctor's case and it was not in Parker's.

MR. SMITH: Then Mackenzie is not a good doctor. The operation should have succeeded with both of them or else both should have died.

Thus, the play shows a reality in which incoherence is at work in a conventional context. In this case, content is 'made strange'. The audience is confronted with an alienated communication exchange that leads them to question their own.

Similarly, the play ends with the following indication:

> *[The words cease abruptly. Again, the lights come on. Mr. and Mrs. Martin are seated like the Smiths at the beginning of the play. The play begins again with the Martins, who say exactly the same lines as the Smiths in the first scene, while the curtain softly falls.]*

The end is no-end. This contradiction is materialised in an unbroken ring present throughout the whole play. This is a technique of Defamiliarisation that breaks with plot conventions and as a result leads to several interpretations. For instance, that the absurd is a never-ending flow of misunderstandings that operates as a logic and coherent system of social communication.

In sum, the study of semiotics assist in understanding the power of theatre as tool to persuade, dominate or contest. Greek tragedy consolidates the notions of Empathia and Catharsis, which create a submissive spectator. Brecht's thesis asserts that the stage is not the world and the spectator has to step back and become a critical observer. There are a number of techniques to dismantle the belief that dramatic conventions are natural and timeless. These techniques feed the spectator's critical abilities by disrupting stage and script habits.

Chapter 2   Theatre of the Oppressed

This chapter looks at Augusto Boal's Theatre of the Oppressed, the context in which it developed and its current impact in the international arena. His work draws from Brecht's techniques and Paulo Freire's 'Pedagogy of the Oppressed'.[25]

The Theatre of the Oppressed attempts to give a voice to the voiceless by promoting dialogue instead of monologue. A system of techniques that revolts against uncontested structures of power and oppression. Boal distances his theatre from conventional and classic forms of drama and suggests new forms of performance that do not reproduce ruling ideologies. Similarly, Boal contests Aristotle's catharsis and encourages the audience to actively engage with the people onstage.

Boal puts forward an arena of real action rather than a fiction of action. Boal's aesthetic language appeared in a Brazil's pre-military coup environment. For this reason Boal was kidnapped, arrested, tortured and exiled to Argentina, then to Europe spreading a particular form of revolution. Theatre is a language with no limits. Boal conceives it as a vehicle for self-expression that contests repressive boundaries. The actors and non-actors that play by Boal's rules have the chance to establish dialectic relationships with their communities and the societies they belong to. They also gain a better understanding of their role and position in their everyday scene. The Theatre of the Oppressed allows the rehearsals of a real life transformation.

Augusto Boal, Text and Context

Brazilian born Augusto Boal is a theatre practitioner and implementer of the Theatre of the Oppressed. He received a degree in Chemical engineering in the early 1950s from Columbia

---

[25] Paulo Freire, *Pedagogy of the Oppressed* (London: Routledge, 1970)

University. On his return to Brazil he worked at the Arena Theatre in Sao Paulo where he introduced and developed innovative theatre techniques associated to political activism.[26]

In order to understand Boal's work it is essential to look at the time and context in which the Theatre of the Oppressed originated. Latin-America's 60s, 70s and 80s witnessed the starting point and growth of a political theatre that started with the Cuban revolution and followed subsequent military dictatorships across the continent. Indeed, the development of the TO took place in a number of Latin American countries in a highly violent social and political climate.[27]

The 1970s saw the rise and expansion of extreme right ideology and dictatorships across most of Latin American countries. Indeed, from the 1960s to the 1980s Latin American dictators worked collaboratively founding an international repressive organisation that would pursue regime opponents beyond physical boundaries. Any dissident or oppositional voice was considered enemy of the dictatorial government. As an example, members of the socialist and communist parties were considered enemies. The military regime legitimated the slaughter of its enemies and therefore violated human rights constantly. Thus, repression was implemented through illegal detentions, kidnapping, manslaughter and torture of victims. Brazil's most bloody and violent years were found at the end of the 1970s. Soon after constitutional systems were abolished in Argentina, Chile and Uruguay the violation of human rights was the population's everyday life. These dictatorships and their methods to control subversion were supported by the US government, later on identified by Boal as an 'Oppressor'.

---

[26] Boal's biography available at Pedagogy and Theare of the Oppressed website:
http://ptoweb.org/aboutpto/a-brief-biography-of-augusto-boal/
[27] Information available at: http://www.rmm.cl/index_sub2.php?id_contenido=5649&id-seccion=387&id_portal=86

Boal's work started in the early 70s and focused on Latin America's particular conditions of oppression. His concept of oppression is related to Paulo Freire's culture of silence. Freire explains that silencing is a form of coercive power and describes how parts of the Brazilian population are socially mute and excluded.

In the early 1970s Boal worked mainly with poor communities. Some of this work centred on communities of illiterate people. Thus, in this case the challenge is to provide people with a system of symbols that can pair the written and spoken language. In a workshop carried out in Peru in the 1970s Boal explores the medium of photography as a straightforward means of communication in which there is no possible ambiguity concerning the semiotics of signs. As he states:

> 'The use of photography may help to discover valid symbols for a whole community or social group. It happens many times that well intentioned theatrical groups are unable to communicate with a mass audience because they use symbols that are meaningless for that audience.'[28]

Boal's assertion explains the need for adapting to the audience and finding a middle ground where communication is efficient in establishing a meaningful dialogue. This idea opposes the principle of imposing one elitist language where the audience is transformed into passive onlookers. Indeed, Boal looks at Greek tragedy as a consolidating a hierarchy in which 'the ruling class took possession of the theatre and built their walls. First, they divided the people, separating actors from spectators: people who act and people who watch (...) Secondly, among the actors, they separated the protagonists from the mass. The coercive indoctrination began!'[29]

---

[28] Augusto Boal *Theatre of the Oppressed* (London: Pluto Press, 1979), 124
[29] Augusto Boal Theatre of the Oppressed (London: Pluto Press, 1979), 119

One of the workshops Boal carried out consisted of getting people talking about their environment. This workshop took place in Peru and people were asked in Spanish to talk about their 'home'. People responded in 'photography' and brought pictures that represented their idea of home. The assortment of images included shacks, rats, wild dogs and so on.[30] Speaking in 'photography' is the first step to express one's reality in a symbolic language that might allow exploring and working on further changes.

Baz Kershaw (1992) mentions this type of theatre that uses different methods to raise questions and pinpoint issues that are directly related and/or affecting its public, since:

> 'a theatre committed to bringing about actual change in specific communities. The companies making this theatre combine art and action, aesthetics and pragmatics. Dealing with material-stories, documentary information, image and so on-inscribed with questions of importance to their audiences'.[31]

Theatre of the Oppressed as a language

Paulo Freire's work has influenced all those working with the oppressed. In his 'Pedagogy of the Oppressed' Freire examines the nature of the relationship oppressor/oppressed. At the core of his work is the concept of conscientization. This is the process of building an awareness, a consciousness that has the ability to change reality. Freire conceives education as a two-way process where people expand their horizon through dialogue. The ultimate aim of education is the praxis of freedom. Freire brings up and analyses the 'generative themes' that open the process of conscientization.

---

[30] *Ibid.*
[31] Baz Kershaw *The Politics of Performance* (London: Routledge, 1992), 5

Once the dialogue is found and communication is possible the next step is to become an agent of change, at least during the TO's sessions. As Boal explains: 'In a Theatre of the Oppressed session, there are no spectators, only *active observers* (or spect-actors).[32]

Similarly, Forum Theatre, one of the TO's techniques that will be further explained, is a flexible language that has to be adapted to its audience.

Forum Theatre is one of the stages of Boal's TO in which the spectator becomes 'spect-actor'. The process is summarised in the following figure:[33]

First stage: Knowing the body

Second stage: Making the body expressive

Third stage: The theatre as language

    First degree: Simultaneous dramaturgy

    Second degree: Image theatre

    Third degree: Forum Theatre

Fourth stage: The theatre as discourse

The first stage, knowing the body, is about understanding the body as a means of expression, 'its social distortions and possibilities of rehabilitation'[34] The second stage, making the body expressive, explores new and unusual ways of personal expression through the body.

The third stage, the theatre as language, is at the core of the TO. As shown in the above diagram this stage comprises three other sub-groups. Simultaneous dramaturgy is the first

---

[32] Augusto Boal "The cop in the Head Three Hypotheses" *The Drama Review* 34, n 2 (T127), Fall 1990
[33] Augusto Boal Theatre of the Oppressed (London: Pluto Press, 1979), 126
[34] Augusto Boal Theatre of the Oppressed (London: Pluto Press, 1979), 126

degree in which the audience is gradually integrated with the on-going action on stage. This degree consists of performing a short scene whether following a script or improvised that looks at a particular problem relevant for the community. Through their performance the actors introduce the conflict, and then they ask the audience for answers. They play and improvise the solutions suggested by the audience who in this case act as playwrights.

The second degree is Image theatre. This is a highly symbolic degree where the audience is more actively involved with the action on stage. Talk is forbidden. It is all about speaking through the actor's bodies. Thus the audience, in this case acting as stage directors, can visually arrange the scene in a way that an issue like 'Imperialism' is displayed and open to discussion on stage. Here they are dealing with *actual images* and *ideal images*. The *actual image* introduces a situation. The *ideal image* offers different options to solve the conflict represented in the *actual image*. Similarly, there is a *transitional* image, which represents the transformation, the change, the middle stage between one reality and another. The third degree is Forum Theatre, the most widespread TO technique. This is about playing a scene of political or social relevance and suggesting solutions. The suggested solution is performed, here the novelty is that any member of the audience can replace an actor and lead the scene, suggesting alternative answers. Thus, the change is not made from the seat but on stage, performing action. Very often the spectator-actor realises that things are not as easy to carry out.

The following quote summarises very well the previous stages and the essence and ultimate aim of the procedure since:

> It is an enormous advance not to let oneself be invaded by the characters. We don't allow ourselves to be invaded, but-is that all there is to it? Should actors and characters go on dominating the stage, their domain, while I am still in the audience? I

think not. I think we could go much further: we need to invade! The audience mustn't just liberate its critical conscience, but its body too. It needs to invade the stage and transform the images that are shown there.'[35]

Forum Theatre dismisses the cathartic element. In conventional theatre the audience vicariously experiences the actions performed on stage. Thus, if the protagonist wins on stage, the audience feels victorious. Then, there is no need for struggle and fight in real life since the illusion of victory already governs the minds of the audience. Forum Theatre triggers the need for carrying out in reality the actions that are rehearsed in the workshop. In a way, it leaves the spectator dissatisfied, incomplete and subsequently he/she seeks to complete that gap by performing a change in reality.

Geography and performance: TO in different contexts

It is simple to realise that there are significant differences between the political theatre carried out in developing countries and the one in Europe and North America. When working in more industrialised societies Boal deals with the so-called 'cop in the head'[36] and moves towards other 'micro-issues' such as isolation, discrimination and so forth. However, it is important to note that the same aesthetic of resistance is used to sort different conflicts out. The issues he deals with vary significantly not only in context but in substance: ' (…) the issues of oppression that his work addressed amidst Europe's liberalism were far more psychological, esoteric and metaphysical that those addressed in Brazil, Peru, Bolivia and Argentina.'[37]

---

[35] Augusto Boal Theatre of the Oppressed (London: Pluto Press, 1979)
[36] Cop in the Head: Techniques that help individuals explore the internal voices, fears, oppressions that prevent him/her from living fully. Rather than focus on external oppressors ("cops"), these techniques bring to light the "cops" inside one's head. (http://www.imaginaction.org/index.php?sn=230)
[37] Maddy Schutzman, "Activism, Therapy or Nostalgia, Theatre of the Oppressed in NY" *The Drama review* 34, n3, (T 127), Fall 1990.

Thus, when the TO reaches Europe in the 80s it adapts to a more bourgeois environment in which oppression stands for any situation where there is only room for monologue and therefore, not a chance for discussion: '(…) to speak is to take power: whenever we become the speaker we are empowered.'[38] Thus, the theatre in Latin-America has a more political function than it has in Europe where it seems to have therapeutic effects. It could be argued that in Latin America political action looks at the social macro-level whereas in Europe and North America it is about dealing with the individual's psyche, which would eventually have a consequence in society as a whole. Therefore, the binary opposition oppressors/oppressed exists in both cases, nevertheless the agents epitomising each of the categories vary.

In Europe the oppressor seems to be located within the self since the surrounding system is arranged around an individualistic outlook:

'The post-colonial leisure class with whom he tended to work in Europe were capable of engaging their radical left-wing politics in relative comfort (…) In this bourgeois environment, therapy apparently forfeits its potentially subversive edge and is reduced to a technique for coping- adapting oneself to the so-called demands an affluent and privileged society makes upon an insatiable, capitalist individuality.'[39]

Thus, Boal's aesthetic language meets different needs and demands. The language changes as the speakers change since its reach, effect and meaning is shaped by the context in which it operates.

Likewise, issues concerning infrastructures and funding affect the efficiency of the performance. In developed countries there are funding bodies that support this type of theatre. However, in developing countries the lack of infrastructures is detrimental to the performance

---

[38] Augusto Boal Theatre of the Oppressed (London: Pluto Press, 1979)
[39] Maddy Schutzman, "Activism, Therapy or Nostalgia, Theatre of the Oppressed in NY" The Drama review 34, n3, (T 127), Fall 1990.

since it brings a number of interruptions and complications. Interviewee John Martin, Artistic Director of Pan Intercultural Arts, explains that in India the group has to work in public spaces where it is difficult to get the audience's attention due to the flow of passers-by, animals and the high temperatures. Environmental conditions combined with the lack of funding support makes a more difficult delivery of Boal's method.

Boal, the institution

Boal's theories have made a significant contribution to the field of drama. To a certain extent he has influenced social policy. In Brazil where he has been elected *vereador* or councilman, he has a direct influence on social policy. Certainly, he has introduced the notion of 'Legislative theatre'. Just like in the TO the spectator becomes actor in Legislative theatre the citizen becomes legislator.[40] This brings incoherence to Boal's persona since it seems very awkward to contest the establishment from the establishment's side. On the other hand, Boal has re-introduced and branded innovative dramatic techniques. For this reason, there is a slight feel of marketization of Boal, the brand. Moreover, Boal organises world tours and runs workshops that are around £300 to attend. Ally Walsh, TO freelance practitioner, expresses her concerns on this issue: [41]

> 'I think it's quite hard to step back from yourself and say: 'oh crap! I'm actually an institution myself'. Because it's just interesting, you know, Boal's son is now involved in the workshops… and he is like this travelling institution and he's getting all himself, so maybe his son is trying to kind of take some responsibility away…Julian…but it is kind…it is an institution of Adrian Jackson, Boal and then Julian Boal…and how far away are you from the people that really need your techniques and then, again that's an argument for against the legislative theatre

---

[40] Augusto Boal *Legislative* Theatre (Oxon: Routledge, 1998), 19
[41] Ally Walsh, Interview by author, London 28 August 2007

because the minute you step into those positions of … I suppose… legitimate power or authority or…systems of bureaucracy you are stepping away from the people you think you are representing, I think, so I am no sure that I fully appreciate the extent of the legislative theatre techniques, I don't really understand what he is doing with them, things are a little different.'

Walsh's concerns reflect a fact, and this is that Boal's persona puts in the shade his work. John Martin, Artistic Director of Pan Intercultural Arts, holds a similar argument and finds flaws in the development of the TO. Martin claims that the method has become dogmatic and *Il faut tuer le pere*, that is 'Kill the father', in order to take the project forwards.

To conclude, Augusto Boal formulates a theatre of change in a politically disturbed environment. His radical approach to theatre matches the needs of his surroundings. However, as soon as repression is institutionalised and broadly spread through Latin America, Boal is urged to leave the country. Once in Europe, his theatre serves a more individualised public. In different contexts Boal's method proves as popular.

Within the field of theatre, professionals acknowledge the extraordinary work of Boal and institutions incorporate his teachings to their schemes. At present, Boal is no icon of oppression.

Chapter 3   UK Context, Organisations and Policy

This chapter looks at the influence of the Theatre of the Oppressed in the UK context. It focuses on particular organisations namely Cardboard Citizens, Pans Intercultural Arts and interrogates the rapid spread of theatre companies alike. Similarly, this section looks at the wider framework in which this kind of theatre is circumscribed giving an overview on the history of 'British alternative theatre'. Although this makes up a diverse group the common thread seems to be the driver to break with conventional ways. Similarly, the foundation and development of this movement shows their implication in the broader aim of producing social change in Great Britain. The question that has been raised is whether the distinctiveness of the movement is an apparent contestation or a revolution in its own right. Indeed, as Raymond Williams[42] points out in a number of cases these organisations become absorbed by the same mainstream discourses they challenge. The roles played by these groups in the UK are wide-ranging. Likewise, it is essential to explore the connection between the discourse of change and the provision of funding as well as other policy issues.

Brief History of Alternative Theatre

In order to understand the significance and impact of the so-called 'alternative' theatre in the UK it is useful to look at its development over time. The records of the theatre industry of the 1970s and 1980s are rare. This adds complexity to the task of researching alternative and community theatre of the time. This fact illustrates the funding agencies' overlook on this particular sector. However, this makes sense when considering that the movement resisted the status quo, represented in this case, by the funding agencies. Nevertheless some alternative theatre groups were formerly known as 'fringe' theatre groups. The term 'fringe' first appeared in the 1960s at the Edinburgh Theatre Festival. The festival was a meeting point for original and innovative forms of theatre as well as a ground for debating on drama. 'Fringe'

---

[42] Raymond Williams *Culture* (London: Fontana, 1981),85 quoted in Baz Kershaw *The Politics of Performance* (London: Routledge, 1992), 6

applied to all the theatre groups that were showing something alternative to conventional and recognised theatre.

As an example, the group CAST[43] from London followed this trend and showed an essentially British repertoire. They ascribed themselves to the category of political theatre. At the time, the environment was politicised and influenced by events such as May 1968, the anti-Vietnam war protests and the abolition of theatre censorship. Within this context the number of so-called alternative theatre groups increased substantially. These groups brought ground-breaking content and performing styles to the UK stage. They performed outside the theatre building, on the streets, in the open air where the contact with the members of the audience was closer.

The Arts Council established the notion of 'scale' within the 1970s British theatre. 'Scale' was intended to measure the reach and impact of the theatre companies. Thus, depending on this reach funding would be assigned to the companies. The categories of small scale and middle scale matched the alternative theatre movement. The scale level was decided on the basis of attendance to the performance. However, as the result of a categorisation that prioritised the number of tickets sold, the significance of the movement was lessened. Indeed, this policy and allocation of funding belied the alternative theatre movement with the British theatre industry neglecting the differences and their matching rationales.

What is the meaning of Alternative?

One of the problems that arise when trying to define what kind of groups did the term 'alternative' really stood for since as Kershaw states:[44]

---

[43] Cartoon Archetypical Slogan Theatre founded in 1965 by Roland and Claire Muldoon
[44] Baz Kershaw *The Politics of Performance* (London: Routledge, 1992)

(…) it is not easy to distinguish between groups that were 'alternative' in the sense of being simply theatrically different from mainstream practices, and those that were 'alternative' because they pursued and ideologically oppositional policy.

Likewise, Raymond Williams[45] adds another distinction regarding the category 'alternative' and its wider social framework. He asserts that a cultural contestation does not represent an alternative to current practices and yet, might be taken in as the expression of change:

> 'They represent sharp and violent breaks with received and traditional practice (a dissidence or revolt rather than a literal avant-garde); and yet…they become (in ways separable from the facts of their dilution and commercial exploitation) the dominating culture of a succeeding…period.'

It is important to appreciate that when the alternative practices 'become the dominant culture of a succeeding … period' they are re-contextualised and therefore transformed. This transformation entails a change of circumstance where the alternative practice loses the original oppositional feature that caused its emergence in the first place. As an example, Eddershaw[46] gives account on the use of Brecht in the UK's alternative scene in the late 1970s: Brecht becomes a classic writer, adopted and admired, but simultaneously depoliticised'.

Consequently, in a number of cases the so-called 'political theatre' is de-politicised. When looking at the organisations that implement the TO it is important to consider whether they de-politicise it when it is used as 'the norm'.

Similarly, according to Craig[47] 'alternative theatre' preaches an agenda by presenting a subjective idea of the world's dynamic:

---

[45] Raymond Williams *Culture* (London: Fontana, 1981),85 quoted in Baz Kershaw *The Politics of Performance* (London: Routledge, 1992), 6
[46] M. Eddershaw (1996) *Performing Brecht* (London: Routledge, 1996)

'Alternative theatre almost alone in the past decade has identified itself with the tradition of the oppressed which teaches us that the state of emergency in which we live is not the exception but the rule.'

The state of emergency and the emergence of an 'alternative theatre' to denounce the situation can be related to Mamet's idea that 'art flourishes in times of struggle, and in times of surplus, disappears[48]'. Although it is true that some types of theatre such as the TO appear in response to circumstances of general turmoil, Mamet's idea seems a simplistic view of the origins of inspiration and creativeness. Aleks Sierz states:[49]

'(…) the idea [Mamet's] expresses a powerful myth-the seductive notion that comfort encourages complacency and that a certain amount of discomfort can generate creative solutions'.

McGrath[50] summaries the different dimensions of alternative theatre. These explain the spread and the reach of the movement across the country, since:

Firstly it can contribute to a definition, a revaluation of the cultural identity of a people or a section of society, can add to the richness and diversity of that identity. Secondly, it can assert, draw attention to, give voice to threatened communities, can, by allowing them to speak, help them to survive. Thirdly, it can mount an attack on the standardisation of culture and consciousness which is a function of late industrial/early technological 'consumerist' societies everywhere. Fourthly, it can be and often is linked to a wider political struggle for the right of a people or a section of a society to control its own destiny, to 'self-determination'. Fifthly, it can make a

[47] Sandy Craig (ed.) *Dreams and deconstructions: Alternative Theatre in Britain,* (Ambergate: Amber Lane)
[48] Aleks Sierz "Art flourishes in times of struggle': Creativity, funding and New Writing" Contemporary Theatre Review, Volume 13, Issue 1 (February 2003): 33-45.
[49] Ibid.
[50] John McGrath *the bone won't break: On theatre and hope in hard times,* London:Methuen 1990), 142 quoted in Baz Kershaw *The Politics of Performance* (London: Routledge, 1992),11

challenge to the values imposed on it from a dominant group – it can help to stop ruling class, or ruling race, or male, or multi-national capitalist values being 'universalised' as common sense, or self-evident trust: as such, it presents a challenged also to the state's cultural engineers, in Ministries of Culture, Arts Councils, universities, schools and the media.'

UK Organisations

Cardboard Citizens

Cardboard Citizens is an independent theatre company ran by Adrian Jackson, who has translated several of Boal's books. This company focuses on the specific social issue of homelessness. The company tours several cities in the UK and its plays are performed by homeless people for homeless and non-homeless people. They use Forum Theatre. The company creates customised programs for the participants and suggests different ways forward, '(…) by focusing on participants potential, not problems.'[51] This statement might sound as contradicting the TO's philosophy. However, it could be argued that their intention is to clarify they do not intend to objectify homelessness nor make a source of spectacle of it. The company's *leit motif* is humanising people by removing negative perceptions of labels such as 'homelessness', 'By developing homeless people as professional artists and professional artists as people through a range of experiences it offers.'[52]

The company wishes to bring an in-depth understanding of homelessness to a broader audience. They demonstrate how the social sector can benefit from the arts. Likewise, they set the standards for other companies or organisations aiming at ending with social exclusion.

---

[51] www.cardboardcitizens.org.uk
[52] Ibid.

Pan Intercultural Arts

Pan Intercultural Arts is another London based company engaging with Forum Theatre, 'using intercultural performance work to help facilitate self-expression and promote deeper understanding of our changing cultural identities.'[53]

The company's emphasis is on diversity and celebration of multiculturalism. Although the company's headquarters are in London, the company implements international projects. This organisation uses theatre to create social change. The Arts Council and Bridge House Trust have granted £49,000 and £25,000 respectively in order to support its projects. Indeed, programmes such as 'There ain't no black in the Union Jack' are coordinated by the Home Office and used to deal with social issues related to gun crime.

Policy

This section explores the reason behind the increasing number of theatre companies that promote social inclusion and transformation through drama. Indeed, attention has to be drawn to the rise and gradual occurrence of this type of organisations.

The so-called 'cultural turn in social policy' and 'social turn in cultural policy' explain the current support for art forms that contribute to tackle social problems such as exclusion. Social exclusion can be defined as the dynamic of being shut out from any of the social, economic, political and cultural systems that determine the integration of a person in society.'[54]

Tessa Jowell, former Secretary of State and MP, stresses the relevance of culture in society's development and equates it to other fundamental needs:[55]

---

[53] www.pan-arts.net
[54] http://www.cabinetoffice.gov.uk/social_exclusion_task_force/documents/research/chapters/2.pdf
[55] Tessa Jowell, Rebuilding the Public Realm, Pamphlet, 12/4/05 available at:
http://www.demos.co.uk/people/tessajowell

"Poverty of aspiration" can be as destructive of well-being, optimism and opportunity as material poverty, and that we should treat engagement with culture, in the broadest sense, as seriously, as we do basic standards of housing, community, safety, health and learning'

The Chairman of the Youth Justice Board makes a similar statement and points at the benefits of participatory art programmes:[56]

'Targeted prevention work with the most at risk youngsters in high crime estates cuts youth crime and disorder substantially, improves school attendance and raises the quality of life for those communities. It costs so little money to run [participatory arts] schemes like this, but their impact can be immense'.

The arts and more particularly drama are contributors and witnesses of the development of society. Sawers explains:[57]

'The arts may promote discussion on social issues and the development of social attitudes. This effect is a valuable externality, which relates especially to books and drama. They are the media in which, historically, ideas have been developed and put before the public for discussion; this role for the arts remains important in any free society'

However, it could be argued that given the circumstances some opportunistic organisations might articulate the ideals of inclusion and offer fitting solutions. According to Rolf Hugoson[58]

'the kind of attention that organisations direct to particular problems has been described as an ad hoc adaptation of available solutions to problems that fit those

[56] Chairman of the Youth Justice Board cited in ACE, 2002 available at: http://www.artscouncil.org.uk/
[57] David Sawers "Should the taxpayer support the Arts" Current controversies Num 7, (1993):29
[58] Rolf Hugoson "The rhetoric of abstract goals in National cultural policies" The European Journal of cultural policy vol 3, n 2 (19979): 327

solutions. Policy may appear as a consequence of problems and solutions turning up at the same time and in the same place, as if they were miscellaneous objects thrown into a garbage can'

Likewise, the Arts Council seeks to involve young people with the arts and to promote cultural exchange since: [59]

Collectively the policies will help us deliver the six areas of our agenda for the arts: taking part in the arts, children and young people, the creative economy, vibrant communities, internationalism and celebrating diversity.

Moreover, the Arts Council regards theatre as an appropriate platform to build dialogues within different types of audiences[60]

'Theatre plays a central role in developing living and vibrant communities. We want the making of and engagement with theatre to be at the centre of both metropolitan and rural communities. We want more people to have the opportunity to engage and participate in theatre, to develop and build their creative, technical and communication skills; to engage in debate; and to gain a greater understanding of the world.'

When it comes to funding, the Arts Council supports organisations that can bring innovative solutions to meet the agenda for the arts: [61]

We will fund a portfolio of organisations that are contemporary in their approach and committed to engaging people in their work in new ways. We will continue to review the organisations we fund and priorities those seeking to implement more sustainable

---

[59] http://www.artscouncil.org.uk/aboutus/artpolicies.php
[60] Ibid.
[61] Ibid.

33

business models and to develop partnerships that give their work greater impact and reach.

One of the projects subsidised[62] by the Arts Council is the play 'Nikolina' by Nabokov, 'a new writing theatre company dedicated to commissioning, developing and producing backlash theatre – new work for the stage that offers an antagonistic response to contemporary agendas, trends and events'.[63] This company produces politically charged theatre and this particular play advances understanding of refugee issues. They performed at the Bowen West Theatre, Bedford and Cambridge Drama Centre. Then it went to the Edinburgh Fringe Festival within the Arts Council's East's Escalator initiative, East to Edinburgh[64]

The Department for Culture, Media, and Sport (DCMS) commissioned a review of Research Literature, Practice and Theory called 'Doing Arts Justice'. This review looks at art-form specific models of change to reduce crime. Special attention is paid to Drama and its multiple possibilities. The report looks at theories such as Boal's from a psychosocial perspective:[65]

'Thompson's marking theory (2003) represents an extension of the cognitive behavioural model, linking role and social learning theory with Boal's Forum Theatre (1979, 1992). The behaviour or action ('little dramatic performances') of an individual as a result of an embodiment of past experiences and relationships; a theatre workshop engages with, reveals and can adjust these performances.'

---

[62] Arts Council England awarded Nabokov £45, 175 of GFTA funding in March 2004
[63] http://www.nabokov-online.com/aboutus.html
[64] Escalator East to Edinburgh is one element of the Escalator talent initiative, Arts Council England, East's, ground-breaking artist mentoring project. For the past three years Escalator has supported performers and companies from all over the eastern region in their forays to the biggest arts festival in the world, the Edinburgh Festival Fringe. http:www.artscouncil.org.uk/aboutus/project_detail.php?browse=recent&id=478
[65] P66 http://www.culture.gov.uk/NR/rdonlyres/D4B445EE-4BCC-4F6C-A87A-C55A0D45D250/0/Doingartsjusticefinal.pdf

The DCMS report shows that dramatic art forms are carefully researched and analysed. The information gives account of the potential effects of these techniques whether implemented in combination with others or in isolation.

To summarise, several organisations utilise drama to engage in social concerns. There is a generalised awareness of social inclusion. Indeed, a number of theatre companies specialise in specific subject matters such as homelessness or any other that leads to isolation and social apartheid. This is supported by a social policy and funding bodies that seek social cohesion through these kind of schemes. It is difficult to assess whether organisations are a consequence of the institutions' idiosyncrasy or the path that original art forms are currently following.

Chapter 4 Methods of Research

This chapter looks at the methodology used to research the topic the Theatre of the Oppressed. The main techniques are interrogation strategies, mainly semi-structured face-to-face interviews and the study of previous research and available sources.

All the interviews are semi-structured interviews in a free format. They appear to be informal conversations, however, there is a set objective and therefore follow a 'script'. At the beginning of the conversation, the subject matter is presented to the interviewee. This is a succinct introduction to the topic, the interviewee does not feel the frame is too restricted.

The interviewer uses 'fishing' techniques and asks open-ended questions. This type of interrogation can lead the interviewee to digress in which case; he/she has to be brought back to the original topic of conversation. In some cases, digression can lead to other topics that are equally important.

Ethnography is usually related to cultural anthropology and it is about 'grasping the native's point of view, *his* relation to life, to realise his vision of *his* world'. [66] This is a suitable perspective since the interviewees, in this case the facilitators of the theatre workshops, can share their insight and explain the reason to implement this particular project. The ethnographic interview consists of three steps: A) Explicit purpose, the interviewer explains what the aim of the interview is and takes control of the conversation, B) Ethnographic explanations, the interviewer provides explanations to the informant in order to direct the interview to a precise point and C) Ethnographic questions, questions are introduced by stages.[67]

---

[66] J.Spradley *The ethnographic interview* (Florida: Harcourt Brace, 1979), 35
[67] Ibid.
Jovanovich, Inc

The interviews seek to explore the real possibilities and limitations of Boal's method. The interview starts by asking questions about the interviewee's experience with the method. This is a question that gets the interviewee talking about something they know well and feel at ease to share. Gradually, the interviewee starts feeling comfortable in the conversation and while they give account of their personal experience with TO they unveil their perspective on the topic i.e. One of the interviewees starts talking about his experience and points at the need for long term commitment with the project and how Boal is unable to commit due to his busy schedule.

This is how the interviewee starts sharing the insider's view and progressively engages with the interview without thinking about the answers as 'right' or 'wrong' but as spur-of-the – moment response that need only the appropriate words to trigger the significant statements. At this point the interviewer has to be aware and identify the topics that get the interviewee to elaborate on the subject. The interviewer listens and lets the interviewee speak without interruptions. They have to feel it is a natural conversation. However, the interviewer has to keep in mind the aims of the discussion and try to direct the interviewee towards that goal. Likewise, it is important to be able to foresee how far the other person will be pushed and then raise the controversial questions. As soon as the interviewee starts feeling at ease they will tell anecdotes that are more and more subjective. The person listening will realise when the complicity is established to carry on with the 'confessional tone'.

To conclude, the topic has been explored following qualitative research that includes interviews and the study of preceding research. By interviewing theatre practitioners the insights into the subject multiplied and the conclusive findings determined the structure of the book.

Chapter 5   Practice of the TO

This chapter looks at how different organisations and theatre practitioners work with the TO techniques. Within the field of theatre the term 'Boalian' is used to the extent of replacing Artaud's pervasiveness[68]. Similarly, theatre professionals find Forum Theatre the most efficient language to communicate with the 'oppressed'. The oppressed and their circumstances vary greatly from one context to another. The meaning of oppression has lessened in significance since Boal's first formulation. TO practitioners seem to acknowledge this fact and have different, although not conflicting, views about how to inaugurate a new chapter within the TO. Many point at the powerful figure of Boal and his current status as a guru[69]. Indeed, his persona seems to overshadow his theories and therefore prevent them from evolving. Similarly, others point at the inevitable consequential 'spectacle of the oppressed' and the complications for locating the oppressor. The oppressed are always visible on stage where the oppressor is not. The current arts policy supports the ideas of inclusion, diversity and empowerment of the youth[70]. As a result, a number of theatre companies and organisations adopt the mask of the TO. However, the task of conceptualising 'oppression' is found with difficulties.

There are a number of reasons that explain the spread of the TO. One of them, as seen in Chapter 2, is the suitability of the TO as a vehicle for communication. The practice shows that theatre removes barriers such as 'grammatological density' that exist in speech and complicated dialogue. As one of the interviewees explains the TO works both as an aesthetic expression and as a means of redefining issues, expressing and therefore perceiving a problem from a different angle.

---

[68] Deirdre Gaffney, RADA graduate and playwright talking about Edinburgh Fringe Festival, Interview by author, London, 25 August 2007
[69] See interviews
[70] http://www.artscouncil.org.uk/aboutus/artspolicies.php

In Julia Kristeva's words it functions as a 'carnivalesque language'[71]. This carnivalesque language 'affirm the modern alienated relation of human beings to their world, their art and their language. At the same time allowing them to express a radial and fundamentally revolutionary awareness of this alienation'[72]. Thus, in the TO's case the alienation is the oppression and the expression for it is found through different dramatic techniques. As Ally Walsh, freelance TO practitioner, states: [73]

> Ok, firstly because my colleague and I were working in another language to the mother tongue of the young people. So, we were trying to access cultural wants and not only rely on English or where we did not necessarily have to understand every single word that the person said. In other words, by objectifying the oppression through an image or … still picture they could show us rather than tell us something… and that it might be understood by more than just… ourselves… but it might be an aesthetic way of presenting something.

> So we found that it worked as a starting point but also in performance as well…'coz we were showing to a wide range of audiences. Some people from other countries of (…) other people that did not speak the same language as them… and even some people who did but who were not interested in seeing and hearing the same old problems being spoken about in the same old way. So it was a kind of way of doing something new with the problem.'

---

[71] Julia Kristeva *Desire in language: a semiotic approach to literature and art,* (New York: Columbia university Press, 1980)
In the chapter's section The Carnival: A Homology Between the Body, Dream, Linguistic Structure, and Structures of Desire': 'the carnival [imagine something like commedia dell'arte staged as participatory theatre] first exteriorises the structure of reflective literary productivity, then inevitably brings to light this structure's underlying unconsciousness: sexuality and death' (Kristeva, 78)
[72] The board *Contemporary Literature*, xxiv, (1983):514
[73] Ally Walsh, Interview by author London, 28 August 2007

Likewise, the praxis of TO shows its versatility and the efficacy[74] of Forum Theatre as a tool to communicate. It is a language that listens to its audience and adapts to its needs. This flexibility is not only an intrinsic characteristic of the techniques but a requirement to make it work. These theatrical techniques might fuse with the local ones to reach its public. Thus, in a way, there is a phenomenon of 'glocalisation' in which new dramatic forms are created from an international cultural trend, the TO, and a local cultural practice. John Martin, Artistic Director of Pan Intercultural Arts, explains:

'Forum Theatre is not a formula. It is an idea, and you have to adapt it constantly. If you try to do it in a sort of use formulaic way it'll fail. So, in India for example, we use Bollywood film songs. We change the words to go with the theme. We use local, vernacular traditions. When we do plays in South East London we use rap as a way of getting the kids interested in it. It has to reach out the vocabulary of the audience (…) so you have to merge it, fuse it, hybridise it with the local theatrical modes (…) Non verbal Forum Theatre where they just use a kind of nonsense speak but the situation mimetically is so clear. The people can see what's going on. (…) so you know, sometimes one can get tied down in the language (…) Sometimes Forum Theatre is about what you do not about what you say. It is about the actions you take not the arguments you give. So by working on non verbal, by working on physicality, action that can prepare in a rather different way'.

The idea of physicality and the body is very important in the TO and in theatre in general. As seen in Chapter 2, first and second stages[75] of the TO regard the body. In the TO the conflict is located in the human body and/or between human bodies. The humanist aspect of the TO

---

[74] Alan Read refers to this concept in the interview held on 12 September 2007 when look at the TO
[75] First stage: knowing the body; Second stage: making the body expressive

reminds that of the renaissance. This focus on the human neglects the environment and the effect it infringes upon humans.

Physicality is also connected to the idea of duality. Indeed, self-perception and the image projected to the audience differ. The body can oppress or express. Artists such as Orlan[76] transform their body into a canvas. Orlan explains how the body as a sign is in conflict with one's identity:[77]

> 'Skin is deceiving – in life, one only has one's skin – there is a bad exchange in human relations because one never is what one has. I have the skin of an angel but I am a jackal … the skin of a crocodile but I am a poodle, the skin of a black person but I am white, the skin of a woman but I am a man; I never have the skin of what I am. There is no exception to the rule because I am never what I have.'

Just like Orlan, there is a generalised trend among some artists that perform conflict by cutting their bodies. During his interview King's College Professor Alan Read[78] argues that the ultimate revolution is not conflict in art but to create art without conflict. In this line of thought one can locate the spectacle of conflict as an artistic *mise en scene* of pain. Watching somebody else's pain results in the spectacle of the oppressed. Within this dynamic it could be argued that 'the oppressed' plays the role of the 'the other'. Indeed, the name, Theatre of the Oppressed, assumes that those watching are different from the oppressed. Professor Read argues that 'you do this [the workshop], because it makes You feel better'. Here 'You' means the workshop facilitator or "difficultator" as Boal calls it.[79] This 'You', immediately

---

[76] Orlan is a French multimedia and performance artist whose performances over the last decade have consisted of cosmetic surgery. In 1990 she took the term 'operating theatre' literally and embarked on a projected entitled 'The reincarnation of Saint Orlan', which has consisted of performing – remaining conscious throughout, photographing, filming and broadcasting – a series of operations to totally remodel her face and body, and thus her identity.

[77] Orlan, "I Do Not Want to Look Like …" *Women's Art* 64 (May-June 1995):5-10.

[78] Alan read, Interview by author, London 12 September 2007

[79] When talking about the role of the workshop facilitator Boal (1979) calls it 'difficultator' or 'Joker'

establishes an 'us and them' relationship, which is essentially unequal since the workshop is arranged according to the Joker's gaze. However, some TO practitioners state that Forum Theatre 'doesn't preach an idea, it can never foretell, it is a little bit anarchic'[80]. Even in the academic milieu, as Deidre Gaffney aka Lola Kelly, RADA trained, TV, stage, film actress and playwright explains Boal's work seems to be reduced to the label of oppression:[81]

'Suddenly EVERYONE is oppressed. It's all about oppression. No one seems to pay any heed to the more radical approaches to staging involved with Boal's work, The Invisible Theatre, the inversion of spectator and player, the dialogue, all of that is tossed aside for a grand running commentary on OPPRESSION.'

There is a generalised concern about the limits of the TO and the necessity to take the theory and practice of the TO forward. This discontentment is materialised in expressions such as 'TO is out of date…'[82] and so on, nevertheless, the most experience TO practitioners clarify that:

'Nobody is saying that Forum Theatre changes society. Forum Theatre changes the mind-set of the people who are engaged in doing and watching it so they can go out and demand…Forum Theatre doesn't deliver justice. It does not deliver non-violence. Forum Theatre…It may give you tools. Not universal panacea, it's a way of generating people the knowledge…Only the first step. In some small psychological ways it can make the difference'.

Yet, institutions find Forum Theatre suitable for their purposes. As seen in Chapter 3 there has been a 'generalisation' of the method that has led many organisations to adopt the TO as

---

[80] John Martin, interview by author, London, 3 September 2007
[81] Deidre Gaffney, interview by author, London 25 August 2007
[82] Ally Walsh, interview by author, London 28 August 2007

a strategy to accomplish their aims. John Martin gives account of the recognition of the method and points out that its status is very often more acknowledged than its operation:

'One is that time has proved it, it does work. If you do it well and if you are flexible with it (…) it does work, it's a good tool (…) Not only the theatre workers but the NGOs and the INGOs have also realised that it works (…) ILO, the British Council, Oxfam (…) they are realising that this is a useful tool to get things moving (…) the other thing is 'Oh Forum Theatre, let's do it' there's a little bit of that. But to be honest, Forum Theatre is not easy. And if you are not good at it you'll give up after one or two attempts. Because I've never known theatre which is harder work than Forum Theatre (…) Sometimes there's a misunderstanding of what can Forum Theatre do'.

Furthermore, the adoption of the TO idiosyncrasy might work as an argument to get funding. Some insiders acknowledge this fact by realising that sometimes the managers of social inclusive projects are more concerned about business – related outputs. Ally Walsh elaborates on this point:

'So, I think agenda of inclusion is connected to funding. And I don't think it always…penetrates down to the fundamental beliefs of the organisation. It comes from the Arts Council of England(…) but people go: 'yeah ok we'll create a programme which has to do with access and inclusion' and it doesn't necessarily mean the whole system responds to that. It could be even the people that run that exact project are so more engaged with their own agendas for commercial success, or you know, numbers of audience members or things other than what inclusion really means, which is what are these participants getting out of it (…) not about necessarily making brilliant opera singers out of homeless people. It's saying how can those homeless people get some work and self-esteem and pleasure out of being involved in the project that sees them in a way that's more than just homeless. That's it. And maybe the company doesn't necessarily have the same agenda. And I've seen that myself with the few organisations-that I won't name-that I've had dealings with were…feels like on the one hand the project is all about inclusion and access and …the philosophy behind, everything and the decision that are made later are different to what the project should be focused on.'

Moreover, Walsh gives a particular example that illustrates the fact that the provision of funding might lead to professional malpractice:

'I mean I was at a meeting about five months ago… for arts companies in London that work with young refugees and asylum seekers. And there were about 13 to 15 organisations represented…and they were all newly involved in this kind of work. Why? Because it's more money. And some of them were doing interesting work that is really connected with the individuals and the participants and really respond to what they needed. But others were saying 'this is money, someone else said that is available we should make a project so we can get the money' without saying what do the participants need as a start, before we make the project, before we apply for the funding. They get the money and then they say: 'right, we've got it, so this is…and this is the new group and…that's refugees and then we've got it and we're covered'. Without saying: 'actually there might be specific needs or sensitivities…or …training that we might need to do in order to deal with this group', doesn't happen.'

Gaffney/Kelly talks about the incongruence that currently governs Boal's public persona and analyses his text in relation to his 'celebrity' status:

44

'Boal has made himself an institution and his celebrity status undercuts his viability as a representative of the unrepresented. Boal has marketed himself as the voice for the voiceless. But at this point he is far too established and separated from any sort of voicelessness to be qualified to speak on the behalf of the unheard. Boal's celebrity makes him incapable of identifying with the oppressed he is meant to advocate. Even his early works come off as the well intentioned musings of an educated middle class male with a guilty conscience. His valiant attempts to go in and bring out the voice of the socially and financially paralysed people of Rio were all well and good but they remain a bourgeois boy's charity project.'

Gaffney/Kelly's views are obviously subjective, however, she, as other interviewees identifies the impossibility of long term commitment with a particular community. Certainly, Boal's 'celebrity' status prevents him from following a project from the beginning to the end.

By sharing their view and experience interviewees contribute to the creation of a clearer picture of the universe Boal and theatre of change in general. The interviewees provide subjective options, nevertheless, they also supply first-hand experience of working with the TO and in some cases with Boal himself and/or his entourage. They all seem to acknowledge that practice is always far from the original theoretical framework of the TO.

Conclusion

The Theatre of the Oppressed is an arena that contests the culture of silence. Augusto Boal's theory and practice attempts to get the invisible seen and named. To fully understand the dimension and reach of Boal's challenge it is necessary to revisit basic elements of theatre such as Catharsis, Empathia, audience, actors, performance. Likewise, the different theories and approaches to theatre demonstrate that it is a flexible system of signs. As a system that sends messages and articulates particular discourses, theatre has the potential to be directed for or against the people. This is Boal's thesis. Revisiting Aristotle's and Machiavelli's use of the stage Boal demonstrates that being a passive spectator is like being a silenced citizen. Boal suggests a *passage a l'acte* through drama.

As a mimetic language of social reality, theatre can unmask the interests it serves and challenge hegemonic values. Boal asserts there is no neutral theatre and highlights is rather autocratic character. Inspired by Paulo Freire's 'Pedagogy of the Oppressed' and utilizing Brechtian rhetoric Boal looks for the means to tackle institutionalised relationships of submission. Indeed, his advocacy for freedom and equality coexisted with Latin America's dictatorships of terror. In an environment where the violation of human rights was an everyday legitimate practice the staging of revolution and its mentor were at risk of death. Boal exiled and with him travelled his techniques of change.

Just like Brecht's, Boal's work is thought of Marxist for its emphasis on dialectics. Oppression is found where there is dialectical supremacy. The role of dialogue is to provide awareness. As a general principle, the Theatre of the Oppressed (TO) aims at providing awareness of power relations, however, its uses and interpretations vary from one context to another, from one period to a present one.

Thirty years after its first appearance the presence of the Theatre of the Oppressed is global, serving different conflicts and struggles. From the Integral Literacy Operation in illiterate communities in Peru to the more bourgeois cop-in-the-head, the TO disseminates a wide scope of operation. Nevertheless, the conception of the TO as a multipurpose tool is problematic. In the UK, the TO found a welcoming environment supported by a tradition of alternative theatre and policy reliant on the transformative powers of the arts. The current cultural policy implements a programme of support where different art forms are coordinated and work collaboratively tackling social issues. Theatre is regarded as an art form also able to reduce crime, raise awareness of social issues and empower people. Also, theatre companies can be profit-making and contribute to the social and economic welfare of the country.

As the TO spreads, Boal's persona grows accordingly. The generalisation of the method has shown the need for developing and updating Boal's thesis. Similarly, there is a growing concern among theatre practitioners of Boal's aura, which has eclipsed the project. Some authorised voices claim that somebody else should take Boal's lead in order to enrich the project and meet its original principles and beliefs. Some others locate the project's flaws in its focus on the subject. Displacing the focus of attention from the subject to the object is one of the alternatives suggested.

The Theatre of the Oppressed might have objectified the Oppressed. By placing the oppressed centre stage, by simplifying the world into two oppositional categories. The multiple and postmodern identity that the tool of theatre allows is now reduced to a post-colonial binary opposition that reminds that of master/slave. Who is watching the oppressed? Whose gaze constructs the sentence 'Theatre of the Oppressed'? The oppressed or the oppressor? Or is there still room for third parties? Yes, as Julia Kristeva suggests there is the subject, the object and the abject.

These and many other questions have been raised in this introductory book. A book that acknowledges a general consensus on the significance and efficacy of Boal's work on waking consciousness and transforming the theatre into a sort of *Habermasian* public sphere. Yet, there are some apparent contradictions. It is difficult to assess the life span of the project on a given community or individual. In other words, to identify the closure is equivalent to assess whether change has occurred in a particular community or individual's mindset. These substantial changes do not come about during the few days that the actual Boal's workshops last. Likewise, the expensive fees for these workshops endorse a feel of inaccessibility on a scheme that is meant to promote access.

As Virginia Woolf points in the following fragment where she comments on text awareness, Boal's techniques may sharpen our sense and awareness of the *status quo* assisting the spect-actor in questioning the system he lives in and exploring the possibilities of drama:[83]

> But is it the end, we ask? We have rather the feeling that we have overrun our signals; or it is as if a tune had stopped short without the expected chords to close it. These stories are inconclusive, we say, and proceed to frame a criticism based upon the assumption that stories ought to conclude in a way that we recognise. In so doing we raise the question of our own fitness as a readers. Where the tune is familiar and the end emphatic – lovers united, villains discomfited, intrigues exposed (...) we can scarcely go wrong, but where the tune is unfamiliar and end a note of interrogation or merely the information that they went on talking, as it is in Chekhov, we need a very daring and alert sense of literature to make us hear the tune, and in particular those last notes which complete the harmony.'

---

[83] Woolf, Virginia, *The Common Reader: First Series, Annotated Edition,*(Harvest/HBJ book, 2002), 172

BIBLIOGRAPHY:

Anne Ubersfeld *L'ecole du spectateur* (Paris: Les Ediitons Sociales, 1970)

Augusto Boal *Theatre of the Oppressed* (London: Pluto Press, 1979)

Augusto Boal *Legislative Theatre* (Oxon: Routledge, 1998)

Augusto Boal "The Cop in the Head Three Hypotheses" The Drama Review 34, n 2 (T127), Fall 1990

Alan Read (1993) *Theatre and Everyday Life* (London: Routledge)

Alter, A *Sociosemiotic Theory of Theatre* (USA: University of Pennsylvania Press, 1990)

Aleks Sierz *Art flourishes in times of struggle: Creativity, Funding and New Writing* Contemporary Theatre Review, Volume 12, Issue 1 (February 2003): 33-45.

Baz Kershaw *The Politics of Performance* (London: Routledge, 1992)

Betty Nance Weber and Hubert Heinen (eds.) *Bertolt Brecht Political theory and literacy practice* (Manchester: Manchester University Press, 1980)

Carol Martin and Henry Bial (eds.) *Brecht Sourcebook* (London: Routledge, 2000)

David Sawers "Should the taxpayer support the Arts" Current Controversies Num7, (1993):29

Decon et al. *Researching Communications* (London: Arnold Publishers, 1998)

Elaine Aston, and George Savona *Theatre as Sign-System* (London: Routledge, 1991)

Julia Kristeva *Desire in Language: A Semiotic Approach to Literature and Art,* (New York: Columbia University Press, 1980)

John Fiske Understanding Popular Culture (London: Routledge, 1987)

J. Spradley the ethnographic interview (Florida: Harcourt brace, 1979)

Maddy Schutzman, Activism, Therapy or Nostalgia, Theatre of the Oppressed in NY" The Drama Review 34, n3, (T 127), Fall 1990

Orlan, "I do not want to look like…", *Women's Art* 64 (May-June 1995): 5 -10.

Paulo Freire, *Pedagogy of the Oppressed* (London: Routledge 1970)

Peter Thompson and Glendyr Sacks (eds.) *the Cambridge Companion to Brecht* (Cambridge: Cambridge University Press 1994)

Robert Hewison, R (1995) Culture and Consensus London: Methuen London

Rolf Hugoson "The Rhetoric of abstract goals in National cultural policies" The European Journal of Cultural Policy vol 3, n 2 (1997): 327

Sandy Craig (ed.) *Dreams and deconstructions: Alternative theatre in Britain, (Ambergate: Amber Lane)*

The board Contemporary Literature, xxxiv, (1983): 514

Woolf, Virginia, *The Common Reader: First Series, Annotated Edition,*(Harvest/HBJ book, 2002) ISBN 015602778X, 172

www.cardboardcitizens.org.uk

http://www.artscouncil.org.uk/aboutus/artpolicies.php

http://www.culture.gov.uk

http://www.marxists.org/reference/subject/philosphy/works/fr/saussure.htm

http://vtheatre.net/biomechanics/scenes.html

http://www.ptoweb.org/about/boal.php

www.nabokov-online.com/aboutus.html

http://www.cabinetoffice.gov.uk/social_exclusion_task_force/documents/research/chapters/2.
pdf

http://www.demos.co.uk/people/tessajowell

10612504R10030

Printed in Great Britain
by Amazon